BONE BROTH DIET COOKBOOK:

Recipes to Help Improve your Health, Fight Aging and lose 15LBS in 21Days

By

Betty Moore

BONE BROTH DIET COOKBOOK:

Copyright © 2019, By: *Betty Moore*

ISBN-13: 978-1-950772-27-8
ISBN-10: 1-950772-27-6

All Rights Reserved. No part of this publication may be reproduced in any form or by any means, including scanning, photocopying, or otherwise without prior written permission of the copyright holder.

Disclaimer:

The information provided in this book is designed to provide helpful information on the subjects discussed. The publisher and author are not responsible for any specific health or allergy needs that may require medical supervision and are not liable for any damages or negative consequences from any treatment, action, application or preparation, to any person reading or following the information in this book.

BONE BROTH DIET COOKBOOK:

Table of Contents

INTRODUCTION TO THE BONE BROTH DIET MIRACLE 5

THE BONE BROTH DIET RECIPE FOR A HEALTHY YOU! 7

    Roast chicken stock 7

    Chicken and wild rice soup 8

    Roasted butternut squash, quince and apple puree 9

    Celery root, potato and fennel casserole with walnut-encrusted cod 10

    Fresh chicken broth 12

    Asian-inspired chicken foot stock 13

    Beef stock 14

    Easy Roast Chicken 16

    Roast lamb with olives, preserved lemon and fresh oregano 17

    Salisbury steak for Grown-ups 19

    Marrow Bean Soup with Pale Vegetables 21

    Miso soup with clams and scallions 23

    Beef pot roast with winter root vegetables 24

    Wilted spinach salad 26

    Chipotle Chile, chicken and black bean soup 27

    Cold quinoa salad with radicchio, chicken and pine nuts 29

    Pan-Roasted Chicken with Tarragon and Mustard Cream Sauce 30

    Classic French Onion Soup 32

    Potato leek soup with bacon and fresh dill 34

    Gluten-free chicken and dumplings 36

    Spiced lentil soup with roasted heirloom tomatoes 39

    Curried lentil soup 41

    Onion bisque with frizzled leeks & rosemary 43

    Slow cooker chicken soup recipe 45

    Egg drop soup with duck and aromatic vegetables 46

    Mushroom stew recipe 48

BONE BROTH DIET COOKBOOK:

- Cal do Verde: kale and potato soup with chorizo and smoked paprika 50
- Beef burgundy 52
- **Slow-roasted Duck with Spiced Sour Cherry Sauce** 54
- Kale and White Bean Soup 56
- **Lovage Soup** 58
- Chicken and wild rice soup 59
- **Braised turnips with parsley** 61
- Braised whole baby beets 62
- Chicken Bone Broth - Chicken Stock 63
- **Chicken Bone Broth in a Slow Cooker** 65
- **Fish Stock** 67
- Chicken Bone Broth Recipe 68
- Paleo Grass-fed Beef Bone Broth 69
- **Japanese Beef and Rice Soup** 71
- Beef Short Ribs with Star Anise and Tangerine 72
- Colombian-Style Chicken, Short Rib and Potato Stew 74
- Beef Short Ribs with Porcini Rub 76
- **Short Ribs Provençal** 78
- **Five-Spice Short Ribs** 80
- **Beef Wrapped in Lettuce Leaves, Korean Style** 82
- **Pamela GU rock's Gruenberg Soup** 84
- Molly O'Neill's Beef Broth 85
- Famous Beef Barbecue 86
- Beef Short Ribs with Star Anise and Tangerine 88
- CONCLUSION 90

INTRODUCTION TO THE BONE BROTH DIET MIRACLE

Eating a high-quality, nutrient-dense diet is one of the most essential ways you can maintain a healthy lifestyle and prevent disease. Remember, your gut needs proper nourishment in order to allow your health to really flourish. Bone broth is an easy way to get essential nutrients into your system. You can make it with any animal bones (such as beef, chicken, turkey etc.) which you roast and then simmer with vegetables for hours.

The vitamins and minerals gotten from broken-down bones have powerful healing properties, and can help to alleviate joint and gut pain, boost your immune system, brighten your skin and even make your hair shiny Along with information about the history and varieties of broth.

This Bone Broth Diet Cookbook contains top easy-to-follow recipes for your daily dose of nutrients: collagen, magnesium, calcium, amino acids, potassium, and minerals, among others. Once you can prepare your own broth, it never a doubt that you will join thousands of others worldwide who have fallen in love with that clear, bright flavor that only comes from high-quality and fresh ingredients.

However, the New York Times says it "ranks with green juice and coconut water as the next magic potion in the eternal quest for perfect health." ABC News calls it "the new juice craze." Celebrities like Gwyneth Paltrow and Kobe Bryant are hooked on it. It's bone broth and it's the core reason for this book.

Dr. Kellyann Petrucci a naturopathic physician and weight loss specialist knows the healing power of bone broth. In accordance with Dr. Kellyann's Bone Broth Diet, this book is coupled with delicious bone broth recipes that will enable you achieve spectacular weight loss and more youthful looking skin in just 21 days.

This Bone Broth Diet Cookbook will walk you through the science of why bone broth works, then arms you with a plan to lose weight safely and easily without cravings, weakness, or hunger pains. Bone broth is said to be packed with fat-burning, skin-tightening collagen; has anti-inflammatory properties; helps heal the gut; and warms and satisfies the entire body. You will be introduced to simple but gourmet recipes for beef, turkey, chicken, and fish bone broths and soups that are loaded with flavor and nutrients, and easy ways to cut down on time spent in the kitchen.

THE BONE BROTH DIET RECIPE FOR A HEALTHY YOU!

Roast chicken stock

Yield: approximately ½ gallon

Ingredients

Vegetable Scraps (onion trimmings, celery leaves, carrot peels, garlic etc.)

1 Tablespoon of Cider Vinegar

One Leftover Roast Chicken Carcass (try Perfect Roast Chicken or better still Roast Chicken with Prosciutto and Herbs)

2 Bay Leaves

Directions:

1. First, you pick the chicken carcass clean of useable meat and reserve that for another dish (such as the Asian Lettuce Wraps with Garlic Scapes).
2. After which you add the chicken carcass, vegetable scraps and bay leafs to a crockpot.
3. After that, you pour filtered water over the carcass to cover.
4. Then you add cider vinegar and cook in your slow cooker on low heat for 24-hrs or longer.
5. Furthermore, by adding water to the cooker, you can continue to cook the broth until the chicken bones become flexible and rubbery.
6. At this point, you strain the broth through a fine mesh sieve and pour into mason jars.
7. Remember, that at this point the broth should gel, but it is not necessary.

Chicken and wild rice soup

Ingredients

1-2 Cups of Leftover Roast Chicken Meat

3 Carrots (Peeled and Chopped)

2 Tablespoons of Ghee

1 Teaspoon of Dried Thyme

Salt and Pepper to Taste

2 Quarts of Homemade Roast Chicken Bone Broth

5 Stalks Celery (Chopped)

1 Yellow Onion (Chopped)

3 Tablespoons of Dried Parsley

1 Cup of Wild Rice

1 Tablespoon of Raw Apple Cider Vinegar (or better still Yogurt or Whey)

Directions:

1. First, you soak the wild rice for at least 8 hours in warm water mixed with apple cider vinegar, yogurt or whey.
2. After which you chop or shred the chicken meat.
3. After that, you heat the ghee in pan, when it is hot adding the vegetables and continue to cook the vegetables in ghee until the onions become translucent.
4. At this point, you add the chicken and herbs.
5. Then you continue cooking the mixture for a minute or two.
6. This is when you add the bone broth.
7. Furthermore, you drain and rinse the wild rice.
8. After that, you add the rice to the soup.
9. In addition, you continue cooking until the rice is tender (NOTE: I'm at very high altitude, so this takes a long time for me. Make sure you use your judgment in cooking times).
10. Finally, you season with salt and freshly ground pepper.

Roasted butternut squash, quince and apple puree

Ingredients

One Organic Quince

Pinch of Real Salt as Desired

One Medium-sized Organic Butternut Squash

3 Organic Apples

3 Tablespoons of Coconut Oil

Directions:

1. Meanwhile, you heat the oven to 400 º F.
2. After which you peel, seed, clean and chop the butternut squash into 1-inch pieces.
3. After that, you peel, core and chop the apples and quince into 1-inch pieces.
4. At this point, you mix the quince, apple and butternut squash together so their evenly distributed in a casserole dish.
5. Then you dot the mixture with 2 tablespoons of coconut oil.
6. Furthermore, you bake the mixture until the fruits and squash are fork-tender.
7. After that, you pour the squash, apple and quince pieces into a mixer and, using the paddle attachment, mix until the squash is well blended (NOTE: the apples and quince will remain slightly chunky).
8. Finally, you add the remaining 1 tablespoon of coconut oil, mix again and serve.

Celery root, potato and fennel casserole with walnut-encrusted cod

Yield: 06 Servings

Ingredients

One Fennel Bulb

3 Tablespoons of Ghee

1 ½ Cups of Walnuts

One Recipe Hollandaise Sauce (or better still Herbed Cream Sauce)

3 Medium Potatoes

One Large Celery Root

Six Cod Filets

Celtic Sea Salt and Black Pepper to Taste

Directions:

1. First, you soak the walnuts overnight in blood-warm water and a sprinkling of sea salt (NOTE: Soaking nuts renders them more digestible).
2. Then in the morning, drain the nuts and crush them.
3. After which you set them aside.
4. After that, you slice the fennel bulb, potatoes and celery root as thinly as possible.
5. At this point, you reserve the fennel fronds.
6. Meanwhile, you heat the oven to 400 ° F.
7. After that, you layer the fennel, potato and celery root slices in a casserole dish.
8. This is when you dot the vegetables with ghee and add salt and pepper to taste.
9. Bake for about 25-30 minutes at 400 ° F or until tender.
10. In the meantime, you roll the cod in the crushed walnuts and remove the vegetables from the oven, and put the cod filets on top of them.
11. Furthermore, you pour remaining walnuts on top of the cod.

12. After which you lower the temperature to 375 ° F, and bake for about 15-20 minutes or until the cod is done to your liking.
13. Finally, you garnish with fennel fronds and serve with herbed cream sauce or hollandaise sauce.

Fresh chicken broth

Ingredients

2 chicken feet (preferably peeled with talons removed, if you can find them)

2-3 dried bay leafs

Filtered water (to cover)

One whole pasture-raised chicken (preferably rinsed, cleaned with organs removed)

One-gallon miscellaneous vegetable scraps (carrots, onions, fresh parsley, celery, leeks)

1 tablespoon of whole peppercorns

2 tablespoons of apple cider vinegar

Directions:

1. First, you add the whole chicken to a heavy-bottomed stock pot, cover with vegetable scraps, bay leafs and peppercorns.
2. After which you cover with very cold filtered water into which you've stirred two tablespoons apple cider vinegar.
3. After that, you bring to a boil over medium-high heat.
4. Then you reduce the heat, cover and simmer gently for 4 to 6 hours – skimming off any scum or foam that appears at the surface.
5. Furthermore, after 4 to 6 hours of slow, gentle simmering, remove the pot from heat and strain it through a fine mesh sieve or a colander lined with 100% cotton cheesecloth into jars or bowls to store.
6. Finally, you refrigerate and cool until the broth sets into a firm gel.

Asian-inspired chicken foot stock

Ingredients

1 (2-inch) Knob of Ginger

3-4 Fresh Cayenne (or better still other) Chili Peppers

One (4-inch) stalk of Lemon Grass (it is optional)

1 lb. of chicken feet (with Peeled and Talons Removed)

One Star Anise

One bulb garlic (Peeled)

Directions:

1. First, you add all ingredients to your stock pot.
2. After which you add water to cover and simmer for a minimum of 4 hours and up to 12, adding more water as needed or desired.
3. After that, you skim any scum that rises to the top.
4. Then you strain solids from the broth through a fine mesh sieve or cheesecloth.
5. This is when you bottle and reserve the stock.
6. Finally, you serve in Asian-inspired soups and dishes.

Beef stock

Ingredients

1 freezer bag full of vegetable scraps (onion tops, carrot peelings, celery leaves etc. Don't use brassicas or beets as they contribute an off-taste to the beef stock.)

2-3 Bay Leafs

Several Pounds of Grass-finished Beef Soup Bones (I routinely use 5-8 lbs.)

Fresh, filtered water.

2 Tablespoons of Cider Vinegar

Directions:

1. First, you rinse and clean the bones under clean water.
2. After which you pat them dry.
3. After that, you roast the bones at 400 °F for about an hour until the bones are well-browned and fragrant.
4. Remember that roasting the bones ensures a good flavor in the resulting beef stock (NOTE: Failure to do so may lend a sour or off-taste to the end product).
5. Then once the bones are browned, I suggest you drain off any fat.
6. This is when you add the bones to a big pot along with any vegetable scraps you might have.
7. NOTE: avoid using brassicas (turnips, cabbage, broccoli, Brussels sprouts etc.) as these vegetables will lend a bitter flavor to your stock. Instead, garlic, mushrooms, onions, leeks, carrots and celery add great flavor.
8. At this point, you add filtered water to cover and bring to a boil.
9. Furthermore, once you've brought the water to a boil, add the vinegar and bay leafs.
10. After which you turn down the heat and continue to simmer for several hours (**NOTE:** I usually simmer mine about 24 hours).
11. Throughout the cooking process, I suggest you skim off any foam and add water as needed.

12. Then when the stock is finished simmering, filter through a fine mesh sieve and bottle in mason jars (**NOTE:** The stock should set just like gelatin, and the fat should rise to the top).
13. Finally, you pick off the fat and reserve it for cooking, then scoop out the gelled stock and reheat to serve as soup.

TIPS:

it's wise to serve this stock very hot as it may gel again once it cools.

Easy Roast Chicken

Yield: 6 servings

Tips:

1. Remember, dressing a pasture-raised bird with minimal ingredients enables its rich flavor to shine.
2. However, slow-roasting ensures that the bird is fall-apart tender.

Ingredients

2 tablespoons of unrefined extra virgin olive oil

½ cup of chicken broth or better still white wine

1 (about 4-pound) pasture-raised chicken

Dash unrefined sea salt

Dash ground black pepper

Directions:

1. First, you rinse the chicken and pat it dry before trussing it with 100% cotton cooking twine.
2. After which you drizzle olive oil over the chicken and sprinkle the bird generously with unrefined sea salt and freshly ground black pepper.
3. After that, you place the trussed and dressed chicken into a clay baker or baking dish, adding ½ cup stock or white wine to the bottom of the pan.
4. Then you turn oven to 275 degrees Fahrenheit and roast the chicken, covered, for about 3 hours.
5. At this point, you increase the heat to 375 degrees Fahrenheit and continue roasting for about 30 to 45 minutes.
6. This is when you remove from the oven and allow the bird to rest 5 to 10 minutes before carving and serving.
7. Finally, you save the chicken's frame to make roast chicken stock.

Roast lamb with olives, preserved lemon and fresh oregano

Yield: About 4 to 6 servings

Ready in:

1. First, the lamb is first seared in ghee or clarified butter before deeply aromatic additions of sun-dried olives, preserved lemon, whole garlic cloves and Greek oregano are tossed into the hot skillet.
2. After which it is slow-roasted for several hours to ensure tenderness and flavor.
3. Make sure you minimize dishes by serving the roast lamb in the skillet in which it was baked.

Ingredients

About 2 tablespoons of clarified butter or ghee

1 cup of sun-dried black olives in olive oil

One Moroccan preserved lemon (preferably quartered)

One cup of wine, red or white, or better still chicken stock

1 (2 to 3 pound) of grass-fed lamb roast

One head fresh garlic (peeled with cloves left whole, divided)

One bunch of fresh oregano (preferably Greek, divided)

Directions:

1. Meanwhile, you heat the oven to 275-degrees Fahrenheit.
2. After which you truss and tie the lamb roast with 100% cotton cooking twine to ensure even cooking an attractive appearance.
3. After that, you pierce the lamb roast, inserting about half the garlic cloves into the roast.
4. At this point, you reserve the remaining cloves for the skillet.
5. Then you heat about 2 tablespoons of clarified butter in a cast iron skillet over a medium-high flame until it melts.
6. This is when you add the trussed and tied lamb roast to the hot fat, searing on each side for about 1 minute or so.

7. Furthermore, you reduce the heat to medium and add the sun-dried olives, quartered preserved lemon, remaining garlic cloves and about half the fresh oregano to the skillet.
8. After which you allow this mixture to cook with the lamb, stirring as needed, for about two minutes.
9. In addition, you pour about 1 cup of red or white wine or chicken stock, to the skillet.
10. After that, you remove from the heat and place the skillet in an oven preheated to 275 degrees Fahrenheit.
11. Finally, you roast for about 2 to 3 hours, depending on the roast's size.
12. Make sure you serve in the skillet, sprinkled with remaining fresh oregano.

Salisbury steak for Grown-ups

Yield: 4 servings

Ingredients

Ingredients for the Salisbury steaks

2 shallots (should be very finely minced)

½ teaspoon of unrefined sea salt

2 tablespoons of clarified butter or ghee

1 lb. of ground grass-fed beef

1 egg yolk (beaten)

½ teaspoon of freshly ground black pepper

Ingredients for the wild mushroom and onion reduction sauce

2 cups of dry red wine

¼ cup of clarified butter or ghee (divided)

1 large yellow onion (peeled and sliced thin)

2 cups of homemade beef stock

2 sprigs of fresh thyme

¾ lb. of wild mushrooms (shiitakes, oysters, porcini etc., chopped coarsely)

Directions:

1. First, you toss ground beef, minced shallots together in a mixing bowl and stir to combine roughly.
2. After which you fold in beaten egg, salt and pepper.
3. After that, you continue stirring the meat, seasonings and egg yolk together until the mixture is thoroughly combined.
4. At this point, you form the seasoned meat into four patties and set aside while you begin preparing the mushroom and onion reduction sauce.

5. Bring beef stock, red wine and fresh thyme to boil over a moderately high flame and continue simmering until reduced by half to three-quarters.
6. This is when you melt 2 tablespoons clarified butter in a cast iron or stainless steel skillet over a moderate flame.
7. Then when the butter is frothy, but not yet browned, you toss in onions and fry until they release their fragrance and their edges begin to caramelize.
8. Furthermore, you remove the onions from the pan, and toss in the mushrooms, taking care not to overcrowd the pan.
9. After which you continue sautéing the mushrooms until fragrant and brown, then you set aside.
10. Then melt 2 more tablespoons clarified butter in the skillet and add the Salisbury steak patties to the hot fat searing on both sides until nice and brown on the outside but still pink in the center, then you smother with sautéed mushrooms and onions.
11. In addition, once the wine and stock are reduced by half to three-quarters, remove and discard the sprigs of thyme.
12. After that, you whisk in 2 tablespoons of butter and continue simmering for one to two minutes.
13. At this point, you pour the reduction sauce over the Salisbury steaks, mushrooms and onions.
14. Then you continue to simmer over a moderately low flame until the steaks are cooked through.
15. Make sure you serve hot, with pan sauce.

Marrow Bean Soup with Pale Vegetables

Yield: about 3 quarts

Tips:

However simple and humble, this Marrow Bean and Pale Vegetable soup takes advantage of some of the most charming vegetables of autumn: plump and crisp potatoes, celeriac and parsley root.

Ingredients

¼ teaspoon of baking soda

One large leek, white and light-green parts only, sliced thin

2 quarts of fresh chicken broth

½ pound of parsley root (peeled and chopped into bite-sized pieces)

Unrefined sea salt

1 cup of marrow beans

2 tablespoons of ghee

1 clove garlic (sliced thin)

One-pound celeriac (peeled and chopped into bite-sized pieces)

2 pounds of Yukon Gold or better still German Butterball potatoes (peeled and chopped into bite-sized pieces)

Directions:

1. First, you dump the marrow beans into a large mixing bowl, cover them with hot water by 2 inches and stir in a pinch of baking soda.
2. After which you cover the bowl and let them soak for at least 18 and up to 24 hours.
3. Then once or twice as the beans soak, I suggest you drain away the soaking water and replenish it with hot water.
4. After they've soaked at least 18 and up to 24 hours, then you strain the beans and set them on the countertop for later (NOTE: Discard the soaking water).
5. After that, melt the ghee in a heavy stock pot.

6. Then you stir in the leeks and garlic, sautéing them for about 4 minutes until softened and fragrant.
7. At this point, you pour the stock into the pot, and stir in the soaked beans. Simmer, covered, for 1 hour.
8. This is when you stir in the celeriac, parsley root and potatoes and continue simmering the soup a further 30 to 45 minutes or until the beans and vegetables turn tender and yield when pierced by a fork.
9. Finally, you ladle into soup bowls, and serve hot.

Notes

1. If you cannot find marrow beans, I suggest you substitute with navy beans or cannellini beans.
2. If you cannot find parsley root, I suggest you substitute with additional celery root.

Miso soup with clams and scallions

Yield: About four servings

Tip:

This recipe is one of those special foods – simple and quiet and humble, but also elegant in its simplicity.

Ingredients

1 lb. of fresh clams (scrubbed clean)

6 scallions, preferably white and light green parts sliced thin

2 heaping tablespoons of dried wakame

2 quarts' dashi (or better still fish stock)

¼ cup of white miso paste

Directions:

1. First, you set the dried wakame in a boil and pour enough filtered cold water over the seaweed to cover it by about a half inch.
2. After which, you allow the wakame to sit in the cold water for about ten minutes.
3. In the meantime, you boil or steam the fresh clams until they open.
4. Then as they open remove them to serving bowls.
5. At this point, you discard any clams that do not open.
6. After the wakame has soaked for about 10 minutes, I suggest you rinse and drain it.
7. This is when you heat the dashi or fish stock until barely simmering and add the wakame.
8. Furthermore, you slowly simmer the wakame in the broth for about two to three minutes.
9. After which you remove the wakame and broth from the heat, allowing it to cool for about five minutes before whisking one-quarter cup white miso paste into the broth until it's fully and completely dissolved.
10. Finally, you pour the broth over the clams, garnishing with sliced thinly sliced scallions.

Beef pot roast with winter root vegetables

Yield: 4 to 6 Servings

Ready in: 8 mins

Tips:
Remember that beef and root vegetables are slow-roasted in red wine and seasoned with fragrant thyme for a tender and richly flavored winter supper.

Ingredients

2 ½ to 3 lb. of grass-fed beef rump roast

3 medium parsnips (preferably peeled and chopped into bite-sized pieces)

2 tablespoons of whole black peppercorns

One bunch thyme

One bunch of fresh parsley (chopped fine)

2 tablespoons of grass-fed butter

5 medium carrots (preferably peeled and chopped into bite-sized pieces)

2 medium turnips (preferably peeled and chopped into bit-sized pieces)

2 bay leafs

1 ½ cups of red wine (preferably cabernet sauvignon)

1 cup of beef stock (preferably homemade)

Directions:

1. Meanwhile, you heat the oven to 325 degrees Fahrenheit.
2. After which in a heavy-bottomed, oven-proof Dutch oven or clay baker, heat butter until melted.
3. After that, you gently brown the roast on all sides in the butter and set aside.
4. At this point, you add chopped carrots, parsnips and turnips to the Dutch oven or clay baker.

5. Furthermore, you season the beef and vegetables with bay leafs, thyme and whole black peppercorns.
6. Then you pour red wine and beef stock over the vegetables and meat.
7. After that, you place in the oven and bake, covered, for three to four hours.
8. Finally, you remove from oven and garnish with chopped fresh parsley.

Wilted spinach salad

Yield: 04 Servings

Tips:

Remember that fresh spinach and chicken combine with the smokiness of bacon and sweetness of apples for a satisfying winter salad.

Ingredients

¼ cup of prepared honey mustard dressing

One small red onion (preferably sliced into rounds)

One cup of cooked chicken (chopped into bite-sized pieces)

4 slices of bacon

4 cups of fresh baby spinach

1 small apple (preferably sliced thin)

Directions:

1. First, you fry four slices bacon over medium heat until crispy.
2. After which you remove bacon from the pan, turn off the heat and gently stir ¼ cup honey mustard dressing into the rendered bacon grease.
3. Then you set aside to cool slightly.
4. Finally, you toss remaining ingredients together, garnish with fried bacon and dress with the mixture of bacon grease and honey mustard dressing.

Chipotle Chile, chicken and black bean soup

Yield: 4 to 6 Servings

Ready in: 25 mins

Tips:

This spicy chicken and black bean soup offers a lovely, nourishing warmth when you being surrounded by the chill of winter.

Make sure you serve with cornbread and queso fresco and chopped fresh cilantro.

Ingredients

One yellow onion, chopped fine

¼ teaspoon of chipotle Chile powder (or to taste)

1 quart of chicken broth (I prefer homemade roast chicken stock)

1 ½ cups of cooked black beans

2 tablespoons of butter

1 teaspoon of cumin

1 teaspoon of Mexican oregano

1 cup of prepared salsa

2 cups of cooked chicken (chopped into bite-sized pieces)

Directions:

1. First, in a soup pot, heat butter in a skillet over medium-high heat until melted
2. After which you add chopped yellow onion and fry until translucent, about 4 minutes.
3. After that, you stir in cumin, chipotle chili powder and Mexican oregano into the mixture of onions and butter, continuing to cook for about 1 to 2 minutes.

4. Then you add chicken broth and salsa to the butter, onions, cumin and oregano.
5. Finally, you add cooked chicken and black beans to the soup pot, reduce heat to medium-low and simmer uncovered for approximately 10 to 15 minutes.

Cold quinoa salad with radicchio, chicken and pine nuts

Yield: 04 Servings

Tips:

This recipe is a nutrient-dense, filling winter salad, quinoa combines with faintly bitter radicchio, chicken and salty feta cheese.

Ingredients

1 small head radicchio (preferably chopped)

½ cup of cubed feta cheese

2 tablespoons of pine nuts

Olive oil and vinegar dressing (to serve)

2 cups of cooked quinoa, chilled

1 cup of cooked chicken (make sure it is cut in bite-sized pieces)

1 small red onion, chopped fine

¼ cup of fresh parsley (chopped)

Directions:

1. First, you toss cooked quinoa, cooked chicken, chopped radicchio, cubed feta cheese, and chopped red onion, pine nuts and parsley together until all ingredients are well distributed.
2. Then you dress the salad with olive oil and red wine vinegar

Pan-Roasted Chicken with Tarragon and Mustard Cream Sauce

TIPS:

1. This recipe is simple to prepare, but also rich with cream, broth and a sprinkling of tarragon that balances nicely with the sharp sour notes of Dijon-style mustard.
2. If you don't have time to cut up a whole chicken, I suggest you consider using bone-in chicken breasts or thighs.

Ingredients

2 tablespoons of butter (melted)

Sea salt and freshly ground black pepper

½ cup of dry white wine (or better still vermouth)

½ cup of heavy cream (or better still crème fraiche)

One whole chicken

2 tablespoons of Dijon-style mustard

Several sprigs fresh tarragon or better still 1 teaspoon dried tarragon

2 cups of homemade chicken broth

Directions:

1. Meanwhile, you heat the oven to 400° F.
2. After which you cut up the chicken: Separate the legs and thighs, remove the bone from the breasts, and cut the breasts into 2 pieces.
3. After that, you reserve the back and neck for making stock.
4. At this point, you place the chicken pieces' skin side up in a stainless steel roasting pan.
5. Then in a small bowl, you combine the melted butter and mustard and brush the skin of the chicken with the mixture.
6. Sprinkle with salt and pepper, then strew the tarragon over the top.
7. Bake for an hour, until the chicken is cooked through and browned on the outside.
8. This is when you remove the chicken pieces to a platter and keep them warm.

9. Furthermore, you place the baking pan over medium heat and deglaze the pan with the wine, stirring to remove any browned bits from the bottom of the pan.
10. After that, you add the broth, bring to a boil, and boil until reduced by about half.
11. Then you gradually add the cream and boil to reduce it a little more, until a thick sauce consistency is reached.
12. In addition, you season with salt.
13. Finally, you strain the sauce into a heated bowl or gravy boat and serve with the chicken.

Classic French Onion Soup
Tips:

However, sweet with the flavor of long-simmered onions, this recipe also takes a savory note from reduced beef stock, bay, black peppercorns and thyme.

Ingredients

One-pound yellow onions (peeled and sliced thin)

¼ pound shallots (peeled and sliced thin)

2 bay leaves

1 teaspoon of smoked black peppercorns

1 cup of dry white wine

4 ounces of Gruyere cheese (shredded)

One tablespoon of grass-fed beef tallow

¾ pound of red onions (peeled and sliced thin)

1 teaspoon of unrefined sea salt

3 sprigs thyme

1 ½ quarts of beef stock

4 slices of day-old sourdough bread

Directions:

1. First, you melt the tallow in a heavy-bottomed stock pot over medium-high heat, then stir in onions and shallots.
2. After which you reduce the heat to medium-low and stir in salt.
3. After that, you cover and sweat the alliums, stirring frequently, about 10 minutes until softened and translucent.

4. Then while the alliums sweat, tie bay leaves, thyme and peppercorns together in a piece of cheesecloth or a small muslin bag, and add it to the pot.
5. At this point, you stir in beef stock and wine, then simmer, uncovered, for 20 to 30 minutes or until the stock is reduced by 1/3.
6. Meanwhile, you heat the oven to 350 F.
7. This is when you ladle into oven-proof soup bowls.
8. Furthermore, you top with a piece of day-old sourdough bread and 1 ounce shredded Gruyere cheese.
9. Finally, you cover and bake for about 20 minutes, then serve.

Potato leek soup with bacon and fresh dill

Yield: About 8 servings

TIPS:

1. This recipe truly satisfies and nourishes you on those rainy, cold and wet days of autumn and winter (and spring and summer if you live where I live).
2. Relax and enjoy its smoky, salty bacon pairs with the gentle and subtle flavors of potato and milk while the fragrant aroma of fresh dill brings it all together with a touch of greenery.

Ingredients

4 leeks, rinsed well with white and light green parts (sliced very thinly)

1 quart of fresh chicken broth

2 cups of fresh whole milk

Crème fraiche or better still sour cream (to serve)

4 oz. pasture-raised bacon, fried and crumbled with fat reserved

1 lb. waxy potatoes, scrubbed well and cubed

2 bay leaves (preferably fresh though dried will do)

1 bunch of fresh dill (chopped fine)

Unrefined sea salt and freshly ground white pepper (to taste)

Directions:

1. First, in a heavy-bottomed soup pot, heat reserved bacon fat over a medium flame until melted and sizzling.
2. After which you add the thinly sliced leeks to the melted bacon fat and fry for about five to six minutes or so until they begin to soften and release their aroma.
3. After that, you add one-quart fresh chicken broth to the leeks and dump in the cubed potatoes and cover the pot.

4. At this point, you cook the potatoes, leeks and broth together over a medium-low flame for about 30 minutes until the potatoes are softened and tenderly fall apart when pressed with the tines of a fork.
5. Then you remove the soup from the flame and allow it to cool slightly, then pour two cups fresh whole milk into the soup pot, stirring in the fresh dill as you go.
6. Finally, you season with unrefined sea salt and white pepper as it suits you, then serve the soup with plenty of good quality pasture-raised bacon and a dollop of crème fraiche or sour cream.

Gluten-free chicken and dumplings

Yield: about 6 servings

Ready in: 38 mins

TIPS:

This recipe is rich with broth, fresh herbs and aromatic vegetables, for a bit of variation, consider omitting bacon and adding two cups chopped wild mushrooms(NOTE: any will do, but I'm particularly fond of chanterelles in this dish).

Ingredients

Ingredients for the gluten-free dumplings:

¼ cup of sorghum flour

2 tablespoons of buckwheat flour

1/3 cup of buttermilk

2 tablespoons of butter

¼ cup of finely minced fresh herbs (parsley, chives, thyme, celery leaves etc.)

½ cup of brown rice flour

¼ cup of almond meal

2 tablespoons of tapioca flour

1 egg, beaten

½ teaspoon of unrefined sea salt

Ingredients for the soup:

4 ounces of pastured bacon, chopped

4 ribs celery, chopped

2 boneless, skinless chicken breasts (preferably chopped into bite-sized pieces)

½ cup of finely minced herbs (parsley, sage, chives, thyme, celery leaves etc.)

2 tablespoons of butter

1 medium yellow onion, chopped

4 carrots (peeled and chopped)

1 ½ to 2 quarts' fresh chicken broth

1 cup fresh or better still frozen English peas

Directions:

Directions for preparing the dumplings:

First, you stir brown rice flour, sorghum flour, almond meal, buckwheat and tapioca flour together.

After which you pour buttermilk into the flour and stir the mixture together until it resembles cornmeal.

After that, you set it aside, covered, for about eight hours or overnight.

Then after the dumpling dough has soaked overnight or about eight hours in buttermilk, mix remaining ingredients into the dough and form the dough by hand into balls about one-half to three-quarters inch in diameter.

This is when you set them aside while you prepare the remaining ingredients.

Directions for finishing the soup:

1. **First you m**elt 2 tablespoons butter in a heavy-bottomed soup pot, then add four ounces chopped bacon to the pot and cook it through.
2. After which you remove the bacon from the pot and set it aside.
3. **After that, you t**oss chopped onion, celery and carrots into the pot and cook them until they become tender and fragrant, then add chopped chicken to the pot and cook for 3 to 5 minutes.

4. **At this point, you p**our in 1 ½ to 2 quarts' fresh chicken broth into the pot and simmer the soup for ten minutes, covered.
5. **Then you r**educe the heat to medium-low, uncover the soup pot, add 1 cup fresh or frozen English peas into the soup and drop formed dumplings, no more than three-quarters inch in diameter, into the pot.
6. **Furthermore,** you cover the pot again and allow the dumplings to cook undisturbed for eight to ten minutes.
7. After 8 to 10 minutes, you uncover the pot and stir in fresh minced herbs and reserved bacon.
8. Finally, you ladle into bowls and serve hot.

Spiced lentil soup with roasted heirloom tomatoes

Ingredients

2 tablespoons of apple cider vinegar

1 lb. of eggplant, any variety (peeled and cubed)

2 tablespoons of clarified butter/ghee

3 ribs celery, sliced thin

½ teaspoon of ground cumin

2 bay leaves

1 bunch kale (preferably trimmed and coarsely chopped)

2 cups of green lentils (picked over and rinsed well)

3 lbs. of heirloom tomatoes (halved and seeded)

2 tablespoons of unrefined extra virgin olive oil (plus extra to serve)

One medium yellow onion (peeled and sliced thin)

1 teaspoon of powdered mustard

½ teaspoon of ground coriander

2 quarts of roast chicken stock or better still filtered water

Directions:

1. First, you pour lentils into a large mixing bowl and cover with hot water by two inches.
2. After which you stir in vinegar, cover with a kitchen towel, and allow the lentils to soak for eight to twelve hours.
3. Then after they've soaked for 8 to 12 hours, drain off the water and rinse them well.
4. Meanwhile, you heat the oven to 425 degrees Fahrenheit.

5. After that, you arrange tomatoes and eggplant on a baking sheet, drizzle with olive oil and roast at 425 degrees Fahrenheit for about 30 minutes or until the tomatoes begin to caramelize.
6. At this point, you melt ghee in a heavy-bottomed stock pot and stir in onion.
7. This is when you fry the onion in ghee until it softens and becomes translucent, 6 to 8 minutes, then stir in mustard, cumin and coriander.
8. Furthermore, you pour chicken stock into the pot over the onions and stir in soaked lentils.
9. After which you cover and simmer for 20 minutes until the lentils are tender.
10. Then once the lentils are tender, you stir in roasted tomatoes and eggplant and continue simmering, covered, for a further 20 to 25 minutes.
11. After 20 to 25 minutes, you turn off the heat, stir in the kale and cover.
12. At this point, you allow the kale to wilt under in the ambient heat of the soup.
13. Finally, you season the soup to taste with unrefined sea salt (see sources), coarsely ground black pepper, and additional olive oil.

Curried lentil soup

Yield: 6 to 8 servings.

Ready in: 11 Mins

Tips:

1. However, this curried lentil soup, perfumed by the luxuriant scent of coriander, cardamom, ginger and fenugreek, provides warmth and nourishment in a single, humble bowl.
2. Make sure you season the curried lentil soup with yogurt, cilantro or fresh lime

Ingredients

½ cup of red lentils

1 teaspoon of coriander seed

1 teaspoon of fenugreek seed

2 tablespoons of ghee/clarified butter

½ inch knob ginger, peeled and finely minced

¼ teaspoon of powdered cayenne pepper

1 teaspoon of fish sauce

Yogurt, cilantro and fresh lime, to serve

1 ½ cups of yellow split peas

2 teaspoons of yogurt, whey, kefir, lemon juice or vinegar

1 teaspoon of cumin seed

6 cardamom pods

2 shallots, peeled and sliced thin

1 teaspoon of curry powder

2 quarts of homemade chicken stock

1 cup of raisins

2 cups of full-fat coconut milk

Directions:

1. First, you pour yellow split peas and red lentils into a mixing bowl with two tablespoons yogurt, kefir, whey, lemon juice or vinegar and cover with hot water by two inches.
2. After which you allow the lentils and split peas to soak for 10 to 12 hours, then drain them and rinse them thoroughly.
3. After that, you heat a cast-iron skillet over a moderately high flame until hot, then toss in coriander, cumin, fenugreek and cardamom seeds, stirring constantly for about 2 minutes until well-toasted.
4. At this point, you remove the toasted spices from the skillet and crush by hand with a mortar and pestle or grind in a spice grinder.
5. Then you melt ghee in a heavy-bottomed stock pot over a moderate flame, then toss in shallots and ginger, frying for about 3 to 4 minutes until fragrant.
6. This is when you stir in toasted spices, curry powder and cayenne pepper, and continue cooking for another minute or two.
7. Furthermore, you pour soaked, rinsed and drained lentils and split peas into the pot with chicken stock and fish sauce.
8. After that, you reduce the heat and simmer the soup until the lentils and split peas are cooked through, about forty-five minutes.
9. Finally, you puree the soup with an immersion blender or run it through a food mill, then stir in coconut milk and raisins and continue simmering for about 10 minutes.
10. Make sure you serve with yogurt, cilantro and fresh lime.

Onion bisque with frizzled leeks & rosemary

Ingredients

2 branches of fresh rosemary

1 head of garlic, peeled and chopped coarse

4 medium yellow onions, peeled and sliced thin

1 tablespoon of white wine vinegar

Ground white pepper (as needed)

2 tablespoons of clarified butter/ghee

4 large leeks (white and light-green parts only, sliced thin)

4 large shallots, peeled and sliced thin

1 quart roasted chicken stock

Unrefined sea salt (as needed)

Frizzled leeks (for dressing the bisque)

Frizzled leeks: ingredients

One large leek (white and light-green parts only, sliced thin)

3 tablespoons of clarified butter/ghee

Directions:

1. First, you melt ghee in a heavy-bottomed skillet over a moderate flame, then toss in rosemary, sliced leek, shallots and onion.
2. After which you sweat the onion, leek and shallots in ghee until fragrant and tender, about five minutes, then remove rosemary and discard.
3. After that, you pour one and one-half quarts roasted chicken stock over the tender leeks, onions and shallots and simmer, covered, for 20 to 25 minutes.
4. Then using an immersion blender, blend the soup until smooth and uniform in texture.

5. At this point, you stir in vinegar and season with unrefined sea salt and ground white pepper.
6. This is when you dress the onion bisque with frizzled leeks just before serving.

Frizzled leeks: method

1. First, you melt ghee in a cast iron skillet over a moderately high flame, then toss in sliced leek.
2. After that, you fry the sliced leeks in ghee until browned and crisp.
3. Finally, you remove immediately from the pan and serve over onion bisque.

Slow cooker chicken soup recipe

Yield: 1-gallon soup

Ready in: 23 mines

Ingredients

Unrefined sea salt, as needed

2 leeks (white and light green parts only, sliced thin)

One yellow onion, peeled and chopped fine

6 celery ribs, sliced ¼ -inch thick

¼ cup of minced fresh parsley

1 whole chicken (about 3 to 4 lbs.)

Ground black pepper, as needed

2 bay leafs

6 carrots, scraped and sliced into rounds ¼ -inch thick

1 lb. potatoes, peeled and chopped into bite-sized pieces

Directions:

1. First, you rinse the chicken, inside and out, then pat it dry and season it well with unrefined sea salt and ground black pepper.
2. After which you place the chicken in a slow cooker with leeks and bay leafs then cover with water.
3. After that, you cook on low for twelve hours.
4. Then you add chopped onion, carrots, celery and potatoes to the slow cooker and continue cooking on low for an additional six to eight hours.
5. Finally, you stir in parsley, pick out large bones and serve.

Egg drop soup with duck and aromatic vegetables

Yield: about 6 servings.

Prep: 30 minutes mins

TIPS:

1. First, you seasoned with ginger, shallots, carrots and scallions, this egg drop soup is deeply aromatic.
2. Make sure you carefully choose a good rich stock like this Asian-inspired chicken foot stock which combines chilies, lemongrass and garlic.

Ingredients

½ pound of duck meat, sliced thin

3 medium carrots, scraped and cut into matchsticks

½ lb. of mushrooms (sliced thin, any will do, shiitakes are nice but I prefer trumpet)

3 scallions, finely sliced

2 tablespoons of rendered duck fat or better still coconut oil

1-inch knob ginger, peeled and cut into matchsticks

2 shallots, peeled and sliced thin

2-quart duck stock (or better still chicken feet stock)

3 eggs, beaten

Directions:

1. First, you melt coconut oil in a heavy-bottomed stock pot over a moderately high flame and toss in sliced duck meat.
2. After which you stir fry the duck meat in coconut oil until cooked through, about 4 to 5 minutes.
3. After that, you transfer the duck meat to a plate and add mushrooms, ginger, carrots and shallot to the pot, stirring frequently until they release their aroma.

4. Then you return cooked duck meat to the pot and pour two quarts' stock into the pot.
5. At this point, you bring to a boil and simmer for 20 minutes.
6. Furthermore, you increase the heat and bring the soup to a brisk boil.
7. Finally, you pour beaten eggs into the pot in a very thin stream, stir the soup and give the soup a stir before garnishing with finely sliced scallions.

Mushroom stew recipe

Yield: about 12 servings

Tips:

This recipe combined with wholesome grass-fed beef and simmered gently for hours in stock, herbs and wine, is a satisfying dish – robust and warming and utterly perfect for autumn.

Ingredients

4 ounces' bacon, chopped fine

6 shallots (peeled and chopped fine)

5 carrots (peeled and chopped)

1-pound fingerling potatoes (I suggest you keep whole if small, chopped if large)

2 bay leafs

2 cups of dry red wine

Unrefined sea salt and black pepper (to taste)

1 tablespoon of clarified butter or better still beef tallow

1 pound of beef stew meat

1 large leek (white parts only, sliced thinly)

5 stalks celery, chopped

2 pounds of mixed mushrooms (button, cremini, shiitake, chanterelle, porcini etc.) (cleaned and chopped)

1 small bunch of fresh thyme

3 quarts' homemade beef stock

1 small bunch fresh parsley, trimmed and chopped

Directions:

1. First, you heat a tablespoon clarified butter or beef tallow in a Dutch oven or heavy-bottomed stock pot over a medium-high flame until it melts.
2. After which you render 4 ounces chopped bacon in the hot fat until it crisps, then remove from the pan and add one-pound beef stew meat, browning on all sides, about 3 or 4 minutes.
3. After that, you remove the browned meat from the pot, adding chopped shallots and sliced leek.
4. Then you fry the leek and shallots in the hot fat until they release their fragrance and begin to caramelize a bit around the edges.
5. At this point, you toss chopped carrots, celery and mushrooms into the pot with two bay leafs and the leaves of one bunch fresh thyme.
6. This is when you fry for 2 to 3 minutes, before deglazing the pot with 2 cups dry red wine and 3 quarts' homemade beef stock.
7. Furthermore, you add browned beef back into the pot along with one-pound small fingerling potatoes.
8. After which you bring the pot to a boil, then reduce the heat and simmer the mushroom stew slowly for about 1 ½ hour to 2 hours until potatoes and meat are tender.
9. This is when you remove the stew from the heat, stir in crisp bacon and chopped parsley.
10. Finally, you season to taste with unrefined sea salt and coarsely ground black pepper as it suits you.

Cal do Verde: kale and potato soup with chorizo and smoked paprika

Yield: About 6 to 8 generous servings

Prep: 60 mins

Tips:

1. This recipe is deeply flavored and brimming with nutrient-dense additions such as manganese-rich kale, potatoes and pasture-raised lard and chorizo.
2. However, for both ease of preparation and for a lovely presentation, I suggest serving the potatoes whole.

Ingredients

1 tablespoon bacon fat (or better still lard)

2 to 3 dried chili peppers

3 to 4 cloves garlic, minced

2 quarts roast chicken stock; I prefer homemade

1 to 2 teaspoons of smoked Spanish paprika

Unrefined extra virgin olive oil, to serve

1 ½ lbs. of fingerling potatoes (preferably no longer than 2-inches)

1 lb. of chorizo

2 shallots, thinly sliced

3 medium carrots, chopped

2 bunches kale, stems removed and chopped coarsely

Unrefined sea salt, to taste

Directions:

1. First, you set a kettle filled with clean water to boil, and boil potatoes until tender when pierced with the tines of a fork.
2. After which you drain the potatoes and set them aside.

3. After that, in the same kettle in which you boiled the potatoes, heat bacon fat or pastured lard over a medium flame until melted.
4. Then you add the chorizo to the pan and fry until thoroughly heated through and well-cooked.
5. At this point, you add the chili peppers, shallots, garlic and carrots to the cooked chorizo and fry with the sausage until they become fragrant and tender.
6. This is when you pour 2 quarts' homemade roast chicken stock into the kettle, and bring to a simmer.
7. Furthermore, you stir as needed and allow the soup to cook for 20 to 30 minutes or so, add the cooked potatoes and continue to cook for another 10 minutes.
8. Then at about 5 to 10 minutes before you plan to serve the soup, turn off the heat and stir chopped kale, smoked paprika and unrefined sea salt into the soup.
9. After that, you cover with a tight-fitting lid and allow the caldo Verde to rest for about five minutes or long enough to wilt the kale.
10. Finally, you serve with a generous portion of unrefined extra virgin olive oil stirred into the soup at the last minute.

Beef burgundy

Yield: 06 Servings

Ingredients

½ cup of Sprouted Grain Flour

5 Organic Carrots, Scraped and Chopped

1 lb. of Organic Mushrooms (Sliced Thin)

3-4 Bay Leafs

1 tablespoon of Whole Organic Black Peppercorns

Bunch Fresh, Organic Parsley, for Garnish

2 cups of Homemade Beef Stock

¼ cup of Clarified Butter or better still Ghee (from Grass-fed Cows)

1 lb. of Grass-finished Beef Stew Meat

5 Organic Celery Stalks, Chopped

2 Organic Yellow Onions, Chopped

Handful Thyme and Marjoram

Unrefined sea salt, to Taste

1 cup of Burgundy or better still Pinot Noir

Directions:

1. First, you melt ghee in pan over medium heat.
2. Meanwhile, you dredge the beef stew meat in the sprouted flour until well-coated.
3. After which you brown the stew meat in the ghee, and remove from the pan using a slotted spoon.
4. After that, you place the meat in a covered casserole, clay cooker or oven-safe Dutch oven.

5. Then you fry the mushrooms in the remaining ghee, and pour them plus any leftover fat onto the stew meat.
6. At this point, you add vegetables, thyme, bay leaf, marjoram and peppercorns to the casserole.
7. Furthermore, you pour in the wine and beef stock.
8. Finally, you bake, covered, at 350 °F for about 3 hours. In the other hand, you may toss ingredients into your slow cooker and cook for 8+ hours.

Slow-roasted Duck with Spiced Sour Cherry Sauce

Yield: 6 Servings

Ingredients

Ingredients for Slow-roasted Duck:

¼ cup of Grass-fed Ghee or better still Butter

1 cup of Dry White Wine (or better still Cherry Wine if Serving with Sour Cherry Sauce)

1 pasture-raised Duck

Unrefined Sea Salt and Freshly Cracked Pepper, to taste

1 Sweet Yellow Onion

Ingredients for Spiced Sour Cherry Sauce:

2 Shallots

1 Cinnamon Stick

2 tablespoons of Honey

2 cups of Frozen Sour Cherries (Pitted)

2 tablespoons of Grass-fed Ghee or better still Butter

2 Star Anise

Directions:

Directions for Preparing Slow-roasted Duck:

1. First, you rinse the duck well and pat it dry.
2. After that, with a blunt butter knife, gently separate the skin of the breast from the meat.

3. Then you spread ghee or better still butter between the skin and meat of the duck breast.
4. Furthermore, slather the remaining ghee or butter along the skin of the duck's breast, legs and thighs.
5. After which you stuff the duck's cavity with the sweet, yellow onion.
6. Then you pour the wine into the roasting pan and roast the duck at 325 º F for 4 hours.
7. At this point, you increase the temperature to 375 º F for ½ hour.
8. Finally, you allow to rest before carving and serving with sour cherry sauce (recipe follows).

Directions for Preparing Spiced Sour Cherry Sauce:

1. First, you heat ghee or butter in a pan over medium-high heat.
2. After which you fry the shallots until they're well caramelized.
3. After that, you add the sour cherries and spices and reduce the heat to medium.
4. Then once the cherries are heated through, add the honey.
5. At this point, you allow the sauce to simmer until slightly syrupy.
6. Finally, you serve with roast duck or roast pork.

Kale and White Bean Soup

Yield: 2 1/2 quarts (6 to 8 Servings)

Ready in: 26 hrs. 5 mins

Tips:

Make sure you save time by preparing the white beans in advance and stirring them into the kale and white bean soup at the last minute.

Ingredients

¼ teaspoon of baking soda

4 ounces of bacon, chopped

2 medium carrots (peeled and finely chopped)

8 cups of chicken stock

One branch rosemary

½ teaspoon of pimento d'Esplette (or better still paprika)

Extra virgin olive oil, to serve

2 cups of white beans, such as cannellini beans

1 tablespoon of butter or ghee

1 medium yellow onion, finely chopped

3 ribs celery, finely chopped

2 bay leaves

Rind of a hunk of parmesan cheese (it is optional)

One bunch kale (trimmed of tough stems and sliced thin)

Directions:

1. First, you toss the beans in a large mixing bowl, cover with hot water by 2 inches and stir in baking soda.
2. After which you soak for 18 to 24 hours, changing the water once or twice.

3. After that, you drain and rinse well.
4. At this point, you transfer the soaked beans into a large stock pot, cover with water and bring to a boil over medium-high heat.
5. Then you reduce heat to medium-low and simmer, covered, for about 1 ½ hours until beans are tender, then drain.
6. Furthermore, you melt butter in a large stock pot until it froths.
7. After that, you stir in bacon and cook until crispy.
8. Then you stir in onion, carrots, celery and garlic.
9. This is when you stir frequently, and fry until fragrant - about 10 minutes.
10. In addition, you pour in chicken stock, add rosemary, bay and the rind of a piece of parmesan cheese.
11. After that, you simmer over medium heat, covered, for about 20 to 30 minutes.
12. At this point, you remove from heat, stir in piment d'Esplette and kale.
13. Finally, you cover and allow the kale to wilt in the residual heat of the soup for about 5 minutes.
14. Make sure you salt as needed and serve with extra virgin olive oil.

Lovage Soup

Yield: 2 quarts (6 to 8 servings Servings)

Ready in: 25 mins

NOTE: feel free to substitute celery for lovage, and be sure to use a good immersion blender to ensure the soup offers a smooth consistency.

Ingredients

1 bunch green onions, white and light green parts (chopped)

2 quarts of chicken stock

Heavy cream, to serve

2 tablespoons of butter

1 medium yellow onion, peeled and chopped

3 medium Russet potatoes, peeled and chopped

1 bunch (about 1 oz.) lovage leaves (chopped fine)

Directions:

1. First, you melt the butter in a heavy-bottomed stock pot over medium-high heat.
2. Then when it froths, reduce the heat to medium and stir in green and yellow onions.
3. After that, you fry for about 5 minutes until fragrant.
4. At this point, you pour in chicken stock and stir in chopped potatoes.
5. This is when you simmer, covered, about 30 minutes or until potatoes are tender.
6. After which you stir in lovage and simmer, covered, a further 5 or 6 minutes.
7. Furthermore, you remove from heat and blend with an immersion blender until smooth.
8. After that, you season with unrefined sea salt and freshly ground pepper.
9. Finally, you stir in a spoonful of heavy cream and serve.

Chicken and wild rice soup

Ingredients

1-2 Cups of Leftover Roast Chicken Meat

3 Carrots (Peeled and Chopped)

2 Tablespoons of Ghee

1 Teaspoon of Dried Thyme

Salt and Pepper, to Taste

2 Quarts Homemade Roast Chicken Bone Broth

5 Stalks Celery (Chopped)

1 Yellow Onion (Chopped)

3 Tablespoons of Dried Parsley

1 Cup of Wild Rice

1 Tablespoon of Raw Apple Cider Vinegar or Yogurt or better still Whey

Directions:

1. First, you soak the wild rice for at least 8 hours in warm water mixed with apple cider vinegar, yogurt or whey.
2. After which you chop or shred the chicken meat.
3. After that, you heat the ghee in pan, when it is hot adding the vegetables and continue to cook the vegetables in ghee until the onions become translucent.
4. Then you add the chicken and herbs, continue cooking the mixture for a minute or two.
5. At this point, you add the bone broth.
6. Furthermore, you drain and rinse the wild rice.
7. After which you add the rice to the soup and continue cooking until the rice is tender (NOTE: I'm at very high altitude, so this takes a long time for me. I suggest you use your judgment in cooking times).

8. Finally, you season with salt and freshly ground pepper.

Braised turnips with parsley

Ingredients

1lb of Organic Turnips

Real Salt and Organic Pepper, to Taste

2 Tablespoons of Ghee from Grass-fed Cows

1 Cup of Beef Bone Broth from Grass-fed Cattle

2 Tablespoons of Organic Dried Parsley

Directions:

1. First, you'll need to peel and chop the turnips into bite-sized pieces.
2. Then while you do that, heat the ghee in a pan over medium heat until it melts.
3. After which you add the turnips and cook (NOTE: They'll brown a bit).
4. Next, you hit the turnips with bone broth and simmer them until they're tender and the broth is reduced into a thick syrup.
5. Remember that bone broth is richly nutritive with its many easily absorbed minerals.
6. Furthermore, you garnish with parsley during the last few minutes of cooking.
7. Finally, you serve warm with mutton or beef for a wholesome, nourishing meal.

Braised whole baby beets

Yield: 4 to 6 servings

Ingredients

2 lbs. of beet thinning or better still whole baby beets with their greens (washed well and patted dry)

2 tablespoons of cider vinegar (preferably raw or four thieves vinegar)

¼ cup of butter (preferably from grass-fed cows)

2 cups of fresh chicken broth (or better still roasted chicken stock)

2 tablespoons of fresh mint (chopped)

Directions:

1. First, you melt butter in a skillet over a moderate flame.
2. Then when it froths, neatly place beet thinning into the skillet so that all the root tips rest in one direct and the greens in the other.
3. After which you sear in butter until the greens are wilted.
4. After that, you pour two cups chicken broth or chicken stock into the skillet, cover, and simmer for about 10 minutes until roots become tender.
5. At this point, you turn off the heat and transfer the beets to a serving dish using tongs (NOTE: For best presentation, lay the beets together so that all the beetroots rest at one end of the serving dish with the greens resting at the other).
6. Finally, you sprinkle with fresh chopped mint and dress with cider vinegar or 4 thieves vinegar.

Chicken Bone Broth - Chicken Stock

Serves: depends upon the amount of water added

Ingredients

2 Tablespoons of apple cider vinegar

4 - 6 stalk celery (chopped)

Water

One raw whole chicken, rotisserie chicken, chicken carcass or parts

2 onions (chopped)

2 carrots, chopped (it is optional)

Directions:

1. **If you are using raw chicken:**
   First, you cover the chicken with water in either a crock pot or stock pot.
2. After which you cook until tender (4 hours on high in the crock pot), remove from water, separate the meat from the bones.

   If you using a roasted chicken:
   First, you separate the chicken meat from the bones.
3. After which you place the chicken bones in a crock pot or stock pot and cover with water.
4. However, if the chicken was cooked in the crock pot covered with water, place the bones back into this water/broth.
5. After that, you add vegetables and vinegar.

Directions for crockpot:

First, you turn crock pot to high until it boils and turn to low - cook for 24 hours.

Directions For stock pot:

1. First, you bring to a boil and reduce the heat to simmer.

2. After which you cook on low for 24 hours.
3. Then you strain the broth and allow it to cool.

Notes:

However, chicken bone broth will keep refrigerated for a week or in the freezer for months.

Chicken Bone Broth in a Slow Cooker

Ingredients:

1 or 2 medium onions (unpeeled and quartered)

2 celery ribs (cut in 1 to 2 inch pieces)

5 sprigs of fresh thyme

1 bay leaf

2 to 2-1/2 quarts' water (just enough to immerse above ingredients)

2-3 roasted chicken carcasses (about 2 lbs. of bones); include any leftover skin or pan drippings

1 head of garlic, unpeeled (cut in half crosswise)

2 carrots (cut in 1 to 2 inch pieces)

5 sprigs of fresh parsley

1-1/2 teaspoons of peppercorns

2 tablespoons of cider vinegar (about 1 tablespoon per pound of bones)

Directions

1. First, you add all of the ingredients to a 6 quart (or larger) slow cooker.
2. After which you cook on low for 12 hours (or more).
3. While still hot, I suggest you use tongs or slotted spoon to remove large pieces from broth.
4. Then you pour through a wire mesh strainer to remove the remaining solid bits.

<u>For a fat-free broth, use one of these methods for removing the fat:</u>
METHOD 1:

1. First, you pour broth into a large bowl or container, cover, and refrigerate overnight or until completely chilled.
2. Then you scrape the hardened fat from the top and discard.

METHOD 2:

First, while broth is still warm, pour it into a grease separator (note: available on Amazon and at cooking stores), that allows you to pour the fat-free broth from the bottom.

FREEZE IT:

However, broth can be refrigerated for about 4 to 5 days. For extended storage, it should be frozen and it's convenient to freeze it in 1 or 2 cup portions for easy use in recipes.

IT USES:

Remember, this broth can be used in any soups, gravies, or any recipes calling for chicken broth.

TIPS: This is a salt-free broth.

Make sure you add salt to taste, as desired.

Fish Stock

Ingredients:

2 tablespoons of butter (organic)

1 carrot (coarsely chopped)

Several sprigs parsley

½ cup of dry white wine or better still vermouth

About 3 quarts cold filtered water

3 or 4 whole carcasses (including heads, of non-oily fish such as sole, turbot, rockfish or snapper)

2 onions (coarsely chopped)

Several sprigs fresh thyme

1 bay leaf

¼ cup of apple cider vinegar

Directions:

1. First, you melt butter in a large stainless steel pot.
2. After which you add the vegetables and cook very gently, about 1/2 hour, until they are soft.
3. After that, you add wine and bring to a boil.
4. Then you add the fish bones and cover with cold, filtered water.

Chicken Bone Broth Recipe

Ingredients:

Chicken necks and feet

Water to cover

3 tablespoons of apple cider vinegar

Sea salt and Ground Black Pepper

2 Bay Leaves

Garlic cloves

Vegetables of choice

Directions:

1. First, you place all ingredients into stock pot and add enough water until chicken is submerged.
2. Then you turn setting to high until it boils, then turn to low and simmer for 24 hours.

Paleo Grass-fed Beef Bone Broth

Ingredients

3 **carrots**

2 **leeks**

A splash of **organic apple cider vinegar**

1 lb. of grass-fed beef bones

3 **celery ribs**

½ head **garlic** (smashed)

3 quarts filtered water

Directions

1. Meanwhile, you heat the oven to 350°F.
2. After which you place beef bones on a rimmed baking sheet and roast for 1 hour.
3. Then while the bones are roasting, roughly chop carrots, celery and leeks into 2-3 inch pieces and add to the crock pot (NOTE: Don't forget to clean the leeks).
4. After that, you cut a head of garlic in half and smash each individual clove of garlic with the side of a knife.
5. At this point, you remove the garlic peel and add smashed cloves to the crock pot.
6. This is when you top vegetables with roasted bones and add water.
7. Furthermore, you set crock pot to high and bring to a boil (NOTE: this took me approximately 4 hours).
8. After which you lower crock pot to low and cook for about 12-48 hours. (For me I let mine go for just over 24 and brought back up to high while I was awake.)
9. Then you use a slotted spoon to remove the leeks, carrots, celery and garlic as best you can then strain the broth through a mesh strainer or cheese cloth into a glass dish or Mason jar.

10. Finally, you let cool on the counter before topping off with the lid and transferring to the refrigerator (or better still freezer, if you don't plan to use/drink within a week).
    Enjoy!

Japanese Beef and Rice Soup

Ingredients

About 10 to 12 ounces shredded cooked beef short ribs (from making broth, or use one pound shredded braised beef)

3 ½ ounces of fresh shiitake mushrooms, stems discarded, caps thinly sliced (about 1 ½ cups)

½ cup of nori crinkles (or better still slice up toasted nori sheets into ½ - inch squares)

1 (about ½ cup) bunch scallions, white and pale green parts only, thinly sliced

7 cups of beef bone broth

1 teaspoon of finely grated fresh ginger

1 cup of cooked brown rice

2 tablespoons of tamari

Juice of ½ lemon

Directions:

1. First, you bring broth to a boil over high heat.
2. After which you stir in meat, ginger, nori, shiitakes, rice, tamari and lemon juice; cook 2 minutes.
3. After that, you stir in scallions.
4. Then you ladle into bowls and serve.

Beef Short Ribs with Star Anise and Tangerine

Ingredients

Salt and pepper

½ teaspoon of ground Sichuan pepper (it is optional)

1 tablespoon of minced garlic

½ cup of tangerine juice

½ cup of dark brown sugar

1 teaspoon of toasted sesame oil

1 daikon radish, about 1 pound peeled (it is optional)

1 cinnamon stick (3-inch length)

3 cups of hot chicken broth or better still water

6 scallions, thinly sliced (for garnish)

5 pounds of beef short ribs (cut flanken style, across the bone in 3-inch pieces)

1 tablespoon of five-spice powder

2 tablespoons of grated ginger

Zest of 1 large tangerine (in wide strips)

6 to 8 small dried Chinese Chile peppers (or better still chilies de arbor)

2 tablespoons of soy sauce

1 tablespoon of salted black bean paste

3 pieces' star anise

¼ cup of Chinese rice wine (or better still sherry)

2 teaspoons of cornstarch dissolved in 2 tablespoons cold water

Directions:

1. First, you season short ribs generously on both sides with salt and pepper and place in a heavy roasting pan in one layer.
2. After which in a mixing bowl, stir together five-spice powder, Sichuan pepper (if using), ginger, garlic, tangerine zest and juice, soy sauce, Chile peppers, brown sugar, sesame oil and black bean paste.
3. After that, you smear mixture over meat and leave to marinate at least one hour at room temperature, or preferably overnight in the refrigerator.
4. Then you heat oven to 350 degrees.
5. At this point, you cut daikon into 1/2-inch pieces and set aside.
6. This is when you bring meat to room temperature.
7. After that, you add star anise, cinnamon stick, rice wine and broth to roasting pan.
8. Furthermore, you cover and bake for 1 ½ hours, then add daikon and return to oven.
9. Bake for about 30 minutes more, until meat is quite tender.
10. After which you remove meat and daikon from pan and keep warm in a serving dish.
11. In addition, you strain braising juices into a saucepan and degrease (NOTE: You should have about 3 cups).
12. This is when you bring to a simmer, then whisk in cornstarch mixture and cook for 1 minute until slightly thickened.
13. Finally, you pour sauce over meat and daikon, garnish with scallions and serve.

Colombian-Style Chicken, Short Rib and Potato Stew

Ingredients

1-pound beef short ribs (rinsed and patted dry)

1 large white onion (finely chopped)

2 bunches cilantro (with roots if possible)

1 ¼ pounds small Yukon Gold or better still red potatoes (peeled and cut into 1-inch chunks)

3 medium tomatoes (cored and chopped)

¾ cup shallots, finely chopped

5 cups of fresh baby spinach

1 teaspoon of black pepper

Sour cream (for serving)

1 whole chicken about 3 ½ pounds (rinsed and patted dry)

2 ¾ teaspoons of kosher salt (plus more for seasoning)

1 tablespoon of dried oregano

2 (about 4 cups) russet potatoes (peeled and coarsely grated)

2 large ears of corn (husked and cut into 1-inch rounds)

¾ cup scallion, finely chopped

1 habanero pepper (plus more to taste)

½ cup of capers with brine

3 avocadoes (peeled, pitted and diced, for serving)

Directions:

1. First, you season the chicken and beef all over with salt.
2. After which you let stand for 15 minutes.
3. After that, in a large pot, combine the chicken, beef, onion, dried oregano and 2 teaspoons salt.

4. Then you rinse away any grit from the cilantro (do not trim), tie one bunch with kitchen twine and drop it into the pot.
5. At this point, you pour in enough cold water to just cover the meat (about 12 cups).
6. Simmer for about 40 minutes until the chicken is just cooked through.
7. Furthermore, you transfer the chicken to a large platter and let cool.
8. After which you stir in the grated potato.
9. After that, you continue to simmer for about 1 ½ hours until the beef is meltingly tender and the potatoes have melted into the broth.
10. This is when you transfer the meat to a platter and once cool enough to handle, shred the beef and chicken, and discard the bones, skin, fat and gristle.
11. Then you stir the chopped potato and corn into the pot.
12. At this point, you simmer until the potatoes are tender, about 20 minutes.
13. In the meantime, in a small bowl, combine the tomatoes, scallions, shallots and ¾ teaspoon salt.
14. After that, you chop 1/3 cup of cilantro leaves from the remaining bunch and stir into this salsa.
15. In addition, you remove and discard the habanero seeds wearing a gloves; finely chop the habanero and add to the salsa.
16. After which you return the chicken and beef to the pot.
17. After that, you stir in the spinach, capers and black pepper.
18. At this point, you cook until the meat is warmed through and spinach is wilted.
19. Then taste and adjust seasoning if necessary.
20. Finally, you ladle into bowls, topping with salsa, avocado and a dollop of sour cream.

BONE BROTH DIET COOKBOOK:

Beef Short Ribs with Porcini Rub

Ingredients

Ingredients for the marinade

2 cups of extra-virgin olive oil

½ cup of honey

16 Korean-style beef short ribs cut across the bone (about 1/2-inch thick, 5 to 6 pounds' total)

1 kiwi (peeled)

2 cups of balsamic vinegar

1 red onion (thinly sliced)

Directions for the porcini rub:

¼ cup of sugar

2 tablespoons of red pepper flakes

4 scallions, trimmed and finely sliced lengthwise, for garnish

½ cup of finely ground dried porcini mushrooms

2 tablespoons of salt

2 tablespoons of black pepper

Directions for the marinade:

1. First, you purée the kiwi in a blender or small food processor.
2. Then in a mixing bowl, combine the kiwi, olive oil, balsamic vinegar, honey and onion.
3. After that, you place ribs in an extra-large zip-lock plastic bag or other large container.
4. Then you add marinade, and mix well to coat ribs.
5. Finally, you seal or cover, and refrigerate for 2 hours.

Directions for the porcini rub:

1. First, in a small mixing bowl, combine ground mushrooms, sugar, salt, red pepper flakes and black pepper.
2. After which you mix well.
3. After that, you heat a grill or broiler.
4. Then you pat ribs dry and slather with porcini rub, coating them well on all sides.
5. This is when you grill or broil for about 2 minutes on each side, or to taste.
6. Finally, you transfer to a warm platter, garnish with scallion slices.

Short Ribs Provençal

Ingredients

2 cups of dry red wine

3 carrots (peeled, in 2-inch lengths)

6 sprigs of fresh thyme

Salt and ground black pepper

1 tablespoon of tomato pesto or paste

6 tablespoons of extra virgin olive oil

2 onions (in 1-inch chunks)

4 cloves garlic (crushed)

1 blood orange, or better still regular juice orange

4 pounds' short ribs (in 2-inch chunks)

1 teaspoon of dried herbs de Provence

Directions:

1. First, in a large bowl, combine 4 tablespoons olive oil, the wine, carrots, onions, garlic and thyme.
2. After which you use a vegetable peeler to cut 3 3-inch strips of orange peel and add them, along with juice of orange.
3. After that, you season with salt and pepper.
4. Then you add short ribs, cover and refrigerate overnight.
5. The next day, you remove meat from marinade and pat dry on paper towels.
6. At this point, you strain marinade into a large measuring cup (Reserve vegetables).
7. This is when you heat remaining oil in a 4-quart casserole.

8. Furthermore, you add meat, a few pieces at a time, and lightly brown.
9. Remove to a bowl and add reserved onions and garlic to casserole, lower heat and cook until starting to brown.
10. After that, you add herbs de Provence.
11. In addition, you return meat to casserole with reserved thyme, carrots and orange peel.
12. After which you pour in 1 ¼ cups marinade and bring to a simmer, season with salt and pepper, lower heat, cover and cook 3 hours.
13. Make sure you moisten with more marinade if needed.
14. Finally, you skim excess fat from surface, check seasoning, stir in tomato pesto or paste and serve from casserole.

Five-Spice Short Ribs

Ingredients

1 ½ cups of dry red wine

1 cup of chicken stock

4 strips of dried tangerine peel (sold in Asian markets), or better still 1 tablespoon coarsely grated orange zest

1 teaspoon of Thai or better still Chinese chili paste

1 tablespoon of minced fresh ginger

1 tablespoon of unsalted butter (softened)

4 pounds of short ribs trimmed of excess fat, bones cut 1 ½ inches long

½ cup of Worcestershire sauce

⅓ Cup of soy sauce

2 tablespoons of coarse brown sugar crystals

1 tablespoon of Chinese five-spice powder

1 tablespoon of minced garlic

Salt and freshly ground black pepper

Directions:

1. Meanwhile, you heat oven to 450 degrees.
2. After which you cut ribs in individual sections, each with one piece of bone.
3. After that, you combine wine, Worcestershire sauce, tangerine peel, sugar, stock, soy sauce, chili paste, five-spice powder, ginger and garlic in a heavy 4- to 5-quart ovenproof saucepan or casserole. Bring to simmer, add ribs and cook for 2 to 3 minutes.
4. Then you cover and place in oven.

5. At this point, you cook 1 ½ to 2 hours, until meat is fork-tender.
6. This is when you remove ribs to a platter, trying to keep a bone in each piece, and cover with foil to keep warm.
7. Furthermore, you strain cooking liquid, and degrease.
8. After that, you return to saucepan, and boil down until reduced by half, to about 1 ½ cups.
9. Then you season to taste with salt and pepper.
10. Finally, over very low heat, whisk in butter bit by bit and pour sauce over ribs.
11. Then you serve.

Beef Wrapped in Lettuce Leaves, Korean Style

Ingredients

½ cup of roughly chopped trimmed scallions, shallots or better still onions

6 cloves garlic (peeled and roughly chopped)

½ teaspoon of ground black pepper

Additional soy sauce or better still bean paste (available at Asian markets), optional

3 to 4 pounds' short ribs

1 tablespoon of ginger, peeled and roughly chopped

1 tablespoon of sugar

½ cup of soy sauce

16 to 24 romaine lettuce leaves (washed and dried)

Directions:

1. First, you use a sharp knife to strip meat from ribs; it will come off easily and in one piece (reserve bones and any meat that adheres to them for stock).
2. If possible, freeze meat for 30 minutes to make slicing easier.
3. After which you combine scallions, sugar, pepper, ginger, garlic, soy sauce and ½ cup water in blender, and puree until very smooth.
4. After that, you slice meat 1/8 to ¼ inch thick.
5. Then you toss with scallion mixture, and marinate for about 15 minutes to 2 hours.
6. In the meantime, you heat a grill or broiler, or preheat oven to its maximum temperature, and put a heavy roasting pan in it.
7. This is when you remove meat from marinade, and grill, broil or roast just until done, no more than a couple of minutes a side.

8. Remember that it is nice if the meat is browned outside and rare inside, but it's imperative that it not be overcooked.
9. If you want to eat, I suggest you wrap a piece or two of meat in a torn piece of lettuce; garnish with a drop or two of soy sauce or bean paste if you like.

BONE BROTH DIET COOKBOOK:

Pamela GU rock's Gruenberg Soup

Ingredients

4 pounds of beef short ribs

2 onions (chopped)

½ teaspoon of freshly ground pepper

1 pound Gruenberg (green wheat kernels), rinsed and soaked overnight

2 beef bones

3 carrots (chopped)

2 teaspoons of kosher salt (plus more to taste)

Directions:

1. First, you put all the ingredients in a pot and add 12 cups water.
2. After which you bring to a boil over medium heat, periodically skimming the foam that comes to the top.
3. After that, you reduce heat and simmer for 2 hours and 15 minutes.
4. Then with a slotted spoon, take out the meat and bones and allow them to cool.
5. In the meantime, you skim the fat off the soup.
6. At this point, you scoop out any marrow from the bones and return it to the pot.
7. Furthermore, you separate the meat from the bones, discarding fat and gristle.
8. After that, you chop the meat into 1/2-inch cubes and return it to the pot.
9. Finally, you season to taste with salt and pepper.

Molly O'Neill's Beef Broth

Ingredients

2 medium onions (peeled and chopped)

2 ribs celery (chopped)

2 cloves of garlic (peeled and chopped)

1 tablespoon of kosher salt

5 pounds of beef short ribs

2 carrots (peeled and chopped)

4 quarts' water

1 cup of red wine

Directions:

1. Meanwhile, you heat oven to 400 degrees.
2. After which you divide the ribs, onions, carrots and celery between 2 large roasting pans and roast, stirring twice, for 30 minutes.
3. After that, you transfer to a stockpot and add the water and garlic.
4. Then you deglaze the roasting pan with the wine and add to the pot.
5. At this point, you bring to a boil.
6. This is when you lower heat and simmer, skimming as needed, for 2 hours.
7. Furthermore, you strain, reserving the ribs and discarding the vegetables.
8. After which you degrease the broth and stir in salt.

9. Finally, when cool enough to handle, you pull the meat off the bones, cut into large chunks and save for another use, or use in soup.

Famous Beef Barbecue

Ingredients

1 (about 4-ounce) piece ginger

1 tablespoon of clear honey

2 tablespoons of minced pear

¼ medium-size onion (chopped)

1 teaspoon of minced garlic

2 scallions (trimmed and halved)

2 tablespoons of sesame oil

2 short ribs beef with bone (about 14 ounces each) or better still 2 (9-ounce) rib-eye steaks, sliced into very thin strips

1 medium-size papaya (peeled and pureed)

3 tablespoons of soy sauce

2 tablespoons of minced pineapple

1 tablespoon of rice wine (sake)

½ teaspoon of freshly ground black pepper

½ teaspoon of sugar, or to taste (it is optional)

½ teaspoon of sesame seeds

Directions:

1. First, in a large bowl or pot, soak the meat in cold water to cover and refrigerate overnight.
2. After which you remove meat from water, wipe clean and set aside.
3. After that, you strain soaking water and reserve 1/3 cup.
4. At this point, you peel ginger and grate against the finest side of the grater, keeping a bowl beneath to catch juices.
5. Then you measure out 1 tablespoon of ginger juice.
6. Furthermore, in a small saucepan, combine the 1/3 cup reserved water, papaya puree, ginger juice, honey and soy sauce.
7. After which you cook over very low heat 10 minutes; do not let boil.
8. This is when you remove and allow to cool slightly.
9. Then in a blender, combine 6 tablespoons of the cooked sauce, pear, pineapple, garlic, pepper, onion, rice wine, scallions and sugar.
10. In addition, you puree until smooth.
11. After that, you stir in sesame seeds and pour into small saucepan.
12. Cook over low heat for about 30 minutes, stirring occasionally.
13. Place beef on a plate, pour 6 tablespoons of the marinade onto plate and rub into beef.
14. At this point, you rub sesame oil into beef and set aside 10 minutes.
15. Finally, you prepare grill and grill meat for 2 minutes on each side, or until brown on outside, for medium beef.

Beef Short Ribs with Star Anise and Tangerine

Ingredients

Salt and pepper

½ teaspoon of ground Sichuan pepper (it is optional)

1 tablespoon of minced garlic

½ cup of tangerine juice

½ cup of dark brown sugar

1 teaspoon of toasted sesame oil

One daikon radish, about 1 pound peeled (it is optional)

1 cinnamon stick (3-inch length)

3 cups of hot chicken broth or water

6 scallions (thinly sliced, for garnish)

5 pounds of beef short ribs (cut flanken style, across the bone in 3-inch pieces)

1 tablespoon of five-spice powder

2 tablespoons of grated ginger

Zest of 1 large tangerine (in wide strips)

6 to 8 small dried Chinese Chile peppers (or better still chilies de arbor)

2 tablespoons of soy sauce

1 tablespoon of salted black bean paste

3 pieces of star anise

¼ cup of Chinese rice wine or better still sherry

2 teaspoons of cornstarch dissolved in 2 tablespoons of cold water

Directions:

1. First, you season short ribs generously on both sides with salt and pepper and place in a heavy roasting pan in one layer.
2. Then in a mixing bowl, you stir together five-spice powder, Sichuan pepper (if using), ginger, garlic, tangerine zest and juice, soy sauce, Chile peppers, brown sugar, sesame oil and black bean paste.
3. After that, you smear mixture over meat and leave to marinate at least one hour at room temperature, or preferably overnight in the refrigerator.
4. At this point, you heat oven to 350 degrees.
5. Furthermore, you cut daikon into 1/2-inch pieces and set aside.
6. After which you bring meat to room temperature.
7. Then you add star anise, cinnamon stick, rice wine and broth to roasting pan.
8. This is when you cover and bake for about 1 ½ hours, then add daikon and return to oven.
9. Bake for about 30 minutes more, until meat is quite tender.
10. In addition, you remove meat and daikon from pan and keep warm in a serving dish.
11. After which you strain braising juices into a saucepan and degrease (NOTE: You should have about 3 cups).
12. Then you bring to a simmer, then whisk in cornstarch mixture and cook for 1 minute until slightly thickened.
13. Finally, you pour sauce over meat and daikon, garnish with scallions and serve.

CONCLUSION

Thanks for reading through this book; if you follow judiciously the recipes outlined above, you will improve your health, fight aging and lose 15LBS in 21Days without effort.

Remember, the only bad action you can take is no action at all.

www.ingramcontent.com/pod-product-compliance
Lightning Source LLC
Chambersburg PA
CBHW081728100526
44591CB00016B/2546